Edward Harper Parker

The Life, Labours and Doctrines of Confucius

Edward Harper Parker

The Life, Labours and Doctrines of Confucius

ISBN/EAN: 9783743373143

Manufactured in Europe, USA, Canada, Australia, Japa

Cover: Foto ©Thomas Meinert / pixelio.de

Manufactured and distributed by brebook publishing software
(www.brebook.com)

Edward Harper Parker

The Life, Labours and Doctrines of Confucius

THE

LIFE, LABOURS AND DOCTRINES

OF

CONFUCIUS.

BY

EDWARD HARPER PARKER.

FORMERLY H. M. CONSUL AT KIUNGCHOW.

(*Reprinted from the* Imperial and Asiatic Quarterly Review, *April,* 1897.)

PUBLISHING DEPARTMENT:

ORIENTAL UNIVERSITY INSTITUTE, WOKING,

1897.

Extract from a Map
published
by Shanghai Catholic Mission
for a book "The Kingdom of Wu."

THE LIFE, LABOURS AND DOCTRINES OF CONFUCIUS.

By E. H. Parker.

In order to obtain a clear notion of our subject, it is desirable to explain who Confucius was, and the condition of the social life amid which he lived. If the reader will look at the map, he will be surprised to see that the China of those days was practically confined to the valley of the Hwang Ho, (which means " Yellow-River "), taken in its broadest sense. I mean that the river which is commonly spoken of as " China's Sorrow," has at different periods entered the sea through channels both north and south of its present course ; has, in fact, taken temporary possession of other river valleys and channels. The China of Confucius' time was, then, confined to the tract of country east of the Great Bend, where the river leaves Tartary for good ; and was enclosed or bounded north and south by the most outerly of those streams which have at any time been connected with the Yellow River system.

We know very little of China previous to Confucius' time (sixth century before Christ), but what little we do know was sifted for us and transmitted by Confucius. We may sum it up in a few words. The written character in an antique form had certainly existed for several thousand years, but it is quite uncertain how many : the best authorities say 3,000, that is 5,000 from now. Very recent discoveries in Babylonia have revealed to us original Sumerian cuneiform records on a wholesale scale, written in clay, and dating at least 5,000 years back ; but there are no such original ancient records in China, nor is there any trace of the Chinese ever having written in clay, still less of there being any connection between Chinese and those western hieroglyphs which preceded cuneiform. Several dynasties had existed, and the rulers of these had shifted their capitals from time to time according to the vagaries of the Yellow River. One of their chief cares was to deal with the havoc wrought or threatened by the floods which resulted from these fluvial irregularities. But although the earliest Chinese literature reaches .back 4,000 years, the older records are so brief and laconic that we derive no satisfactory mental picture from them.

In the time of Confucius the imperial power had dwindled down almost to nothing, and the appanage States of the vassal princes, most of which had been conferred originally upon kinsmen of the King (for the more modern title of *hwang-ti* or " Emperor," which in those days applied to the Supreme God, and thence only by extension to past Emperors, had not yet assumed its present definite form), were almost independent. The condition of China was, in fact, almost exactly like that of France before Louis the Eleventh broke the power of the vassal dukes and counts ; and the position of the Chinese King, as a moral head over all men, was not unlike the present position of the Pope as the moral head of Christendom :

he was towards the end as much a prisoner as a monarch ; his temporal
sway was almost reduced to his immediate surroundings, and the whims of
feudatories, coupled with the infiltration of barbarian customs, were
gradually corrupting the old polity. Not only were the vassal principalities,
dukedoms, and counties insubordinate in relation to the King, but their
own counts, barons, and squires were equally presumptuous towards themselves ; and it was into this chaotic condition of society and policy, where
each clever man was fighting for his own hand alone, that Confucius was
ushered at his birth.

The ancestors of Confucius could, at the time of his birth in the year
551 before Christ, be traced back in a way for over two thousand years ;
but, as we know next to nothing of practical history previous to his time,
it is futile to pursue enquiry into remote family matters. Where nothing
is known of an extinct *genus*, it is vain to enquire into its *species*. The
royal dynasty nominally ruling in Confucius' time began 671 years before
his birth, and one of Confucius' ancestors, who was a half-brother of the
last monarch of the dethroned dynasty, was enfeoffed in a State called
Sung, the capital of which I mark in the map with a cross. About 250
years before Confucius' birth, the reigning duke of this state resigned
his rights of succession to a younger brother. The elder brother and his
heirs were thus for ever cut off from the ducal succession, and the customary law of China then was that, after five generations, a branch of the
reigning family must found a new *gens* or clan of his own. So, then, it
came to pass that K'ung-fu-kia, fifth in descent from the abdicating duke,
gave the first syllable of his name as a clan name to his heirs. The great-
grandson of the man who thus founded in its strict or narrower sense the
family of K'ung was the great-grandfather of the philosopher. In Chinese
the word *fu-tsz* has very much the same meaning, by extension, as the
Latin word *prudens ;* and the *responsa prudentum*, or "legal *dicta*" of such
Roman teachers as Paul, Papinian, Ulpian, and others, were very like the
wise sayings of such *fu-tsz* as Confucius and Mencius. *K'ung-fu-tsz*, or
"the learned K'ung," was too difficult a polysyllable for the Portuguese
Jesuits who first came to China to pronounce accurately, and accordingly
they latinised it into Confucius, or, as most Europeans would still pronounce it, *Confutsius.*

K'ung means a "hole," and, by extension, "a peacock," apparently
because that bird has a number of eyes or holes in its tail. *Fu* means *vir*,
i.e. a man or husband ; and *tsz*, meaning "a child," is simply a diminutive,
just as *homunculus* is the diminutive of *homo*, "a human being," in Latin ;
or as *Männchen* is a diminutive of *Mann*, "a man or husband," in German.
Peacocks were most probably unknown in North China when Confucius
lived, hence his name must be translated "Mr. Hole," and not "Mr.
Peacock"; and Confucius was the seventh of the Hole family counting
from the time when that name was assumed ; or the twelfth of the family
counting from the time when the reigning duke resigned his rights to a
younger brother.

The great-grandfather of Confucius was obliged to fly from the duchy
on account of some political trouble, and he became a citizen of a neigh-

bouring state called Lu. His grandson, the father of Confucius, became an officer of state, and distinguished himself by proficiency in the warlike arts. He was ten feet in height; but the learned are still disputing the question of ancient feet : probably a foot was then 8 inches, as now measured, and Confucius' father would thus be six feet eight inches in height, by no means a very rare thing even with modern Chinamen of the north. This promising soldier had nine daughters borne to him in succession by his wife. In China there can, except under very special circumstances, only be one strictly legal wife, but should this wife fail to present her lord with a son, it was and is still permissible to take a wife of the second class, or, in Scriptural language, a handmaid, who may in certain eventualities hope for future promotion to the full rank of wife. The present Empress-Dowager of China is a case in point. She was originally a handmaid, but after giving birth to the last Emperor, she was promoted in 1858 to the rank of Empress, and for many years acted as joint regent with the Empress-Dowager her senior, who had no children, and died in 1881. It cannot be denied that Confucius' father was very patient with his wife, for it seems he gave her nine chances before he took a handmaid in his despair. This handmaid gave birth to a son, who was a cripple. The gallant soldier was now seventy years of age. In China daughters do not count for so much as sons, and are often killed as useless incumbrances, the great object being to have at least one son to perform religious rites,—those rights which the Romans used to call *sacra privata*. Confucius' father appears to have resolved therefore in his old age to stake everything upon a supreme effort, and he married a mere girl. Either he or she, or both of them, went to pray for a son at a temple on Mount *Ni-k'iu*, a spot which I mark on the map with a circle. The offspring of the union was Confucius, whose personal name was *K'iu*, and whose second name was *Chung-ni* or " *Ni* the Second " (his crippled brother having been the First). The chief feature in Confucius, as a baby, was that the crown of his head was concave instead of being convex, a peculiarity which must have given him a singular appearance. *K'iu* means "a mound," and some say he was so called because his forehead protruded. In China personal names of great folk are tabued, sometimes in writing as well as speech. Hence, if it is ever found absolutely necessary to use the word *K'iu*, the difficulty is surmounted by omitting one stroke, and thus making it a little different. In speech the word "So-and-so" is substituted : thus instead of saying " Mr. Mound Hole," the Chinese say " Mr. So-and-so Hole." There is no tabu to the *cognomen* or second name, and so we have the characters *chung-ni* in daily use. Owing to one historian having used the expression " wild union " in connection with Confucius' mother, some authors have supposed that the soldier "kept company in the wilderness " ; but judicious commentators explain that a man is not supposed to go a-courting after 64, nor a woman to begin it before 14; and that the " wild union " in question did not refer to the absence of due ceremony in the marriage, but to the fact that the husband was unusually spry and the wife unusually precocious for their respective ages. This interesting event took place in the year 551 before Christ;

and two or three years later the father died. He was buried at a spot
eight miles east of Confucius' own grave, as will shortly be explained
in full.

We may pass rapidly over the events which took place during Confucius'
youth. They are of slender importance, and, such as they are, we know
but little of them. At the age of six he was observed to take pleasure in
playing with sacrificial vessels and in imitating ceremonial movements,
much as English children of .the same age sometimes play at holding
church services. He is supposed to have gone to school at the age of
seven, but the best authorities, Chinese and European, are not satisfied
upon this point, which in any case is just what a Chinese boy would do,
and still usually does. Confucius himself informs us that, at fifteen, his
whole mind was devoted to study. What is certain is that his mother
removed with him to the town where his descendants now live : this town
is marked on the map with a star, and is eight miles west of the spot where
his father was buried. In Chinese it is called *K'üh-fu*, or, " Crooked Hill,"
on account of the winding eminence, a mile long, which runs through the
city. About 600 years before Confucius' birth, the first Emperor of the
imperial dynasty of Chow enfeoffed the regent, his uncle, Duke of Chow,
as feudal prince at Crooked Hill, styling this feudal State Lu. It had an
area, or perhaps circuit, of 330 English miles. As we shall soon see, the
Duke of Chow's tomb is still there and Confucius always took him as a
model. Amongst other things Duke Chow invented the compass or
" South-pointing cart." The circumstance of our hero's widowed mother
being a mere girl, and consequently unable, through maidenly modesty, to
follow her venerable husband to the grave, led to Confucius' remaining
for some years in ignorance of a fact so transcendently important from a
Chinese point of view—the exact position of his father's grave : perhaps
matters were made worse by the name of his father's village being transferred to the new residence, just as with us Ann Hathaway's cottage might
have been called Stratford if Shakespeare's mother had taken him to live
there. This circumstance may also account for the conflicting statements
of European visitors as to the exact sites of the existing house and temple
of the Confucius family.

All authorities clearly agree that Confucius married at the age of 19,
that is, after passing 18 new year's days subsequently to his birth ; for in
China, a man born on the 31st December is considered to be two years
old on the following day, whilst a man born on the 2nd of January would
still be two years old on the 31st of December in the following year : so
that there may be 700 days difference between the ages of two people both
nominally in their 19th year. Thus we find, as we go along, that the
simplest Chinese facts have to be tested before we can nail them down
fairly before our eyes and understandings. In Confucius' case the birth
really did take place in the 11th moon, but the next dynasty made some
alterations in the calendar, and what was the 11th moon in Confucius'
time became the 1st moon of the following year a few centuries later : moreover, although we are told the exact day, the accounts disagree in such a
way that there is a discrepancy of some days to account for. All that we

can say for certain, therefore, is that according to our way of reckoning, Confucius was about eighteen when he married.

The next year a son was born, and received the name of " Fish No. 1," with the cognomen of "Carp." This apparently singular choice of names was made in consequence of the reigning duke having sent a congratulatory present of a couple of carp to the young pair. The carp is the king of fish, and no doubt the duke's action had some hidden meaning ; just as, in modern marriages, the Chinese often send a couple of geese as a present to wedded couples : the goose is supposed to be the only creature which does not marry again when its spouse dies. Nothing is known of this son except that on two occasions he is recorded to have suddenly come across his father, and to have been severely questioned as to his studies : he seems to have given his father as wide a berth as possible. The fact of the duke having deigned to congratulate a poor man like Confucius is accounted for by the latter having held, at the age of 20, the post of grain distributor : but here, again, we are confronted with a difficulty ; it is not known whether this means a post in the public granaries, and, if so, central or local ; or whether it means a relief officer. The philosopher Mencius, in alluding to this episode, says that "a superior man may occasionally accept office purely for the relief of his poverty." We may therefore fairly conclude that the duke gave the carp because Confucius was a ducal officer, and that Confucius accepted office, as people do in modern times, to relieve his own poverty.

It is incidentally mentioned in the "Conversations of Confucius" with his disciples that he gave a daughter in marriage. Nothing more. We may therefore once more safely conclude that he had at least one daughter, who, on her marriage, would in accordance with custom cease to belong to his family.

In his 21st year Confucius was promoted or transferred to a post resembling that of estate-agent or watcher over farms ; and a year later he collected round him a number of disciples, much after the fashion of the peripatetic philosophers of Greece. He was six inches taller than his father ; but, if we are to judge of his personal appearance by the pictures and effigies of him still exhibited in his old house, he was far from being a beautiful man, even though he may have been a commanding one. He was strong and well-built, with a large singularly shaped head, full red face, and contemplative, heavy expression. He had a long sparse beard, ill-shaped ears, a thick round-tipped nose, but flat and shovel-like ; two projecting lower teeth, gaping nostrils, and eyes which showed more white than is usual. His back was described by an admirer as being like that of a tortoise. Confucius accepted fees for his instruction, but was more particular about the diligence of the student than the amount of his present. Even at the present day teachers' fees are invariably called "dried meat," or "fuel and water," and schoolboys always make periodical presents of food to their masters.

His mother died when he was in his 24th year. Confucius seems to have buried her temporarily whilst he made inquiry touching the exact spot where his father's body lay : he then opened his father's grave, and transferred to it the coffin of his mother.   Both native and foreign commentators have somewhat confused the facts connected with this event.   None of the Europeans who have visited Confucius' tomb seem to have taken the trouble to pass on to the parents' grave : even the Emperor of China, who went carefully over all the chief show-places in 1684, contented himself with sending an officer to sacrifice for him at the paternal shrine : but the position is quite certain ; it is at Mount Fang, marked on the map with a black circle.   Confucius had to retire from office for 27 months in order to mourn, as the modern Chinese still do, for his mother.   He did this so effectively that it took him five days to recover his natural voice after the 27 months had expired.   During the next seven years he continued his teachings, besides himself studying music, official formalities, and archæology.   His position was much strengthened when one of the leading men in the state commanded, on his death-bed, that his own son and another relative should join the rising philosopher's school.   The duke liberally placed a carriage and pair at the disposal of Confucius, who proceeded in it to the imperial capital in order to make further learned research.   The springless, covered, two-wheeled carts (not unlike a Liverpool market-cart on a small scale), which still ply for hire in the streets of Peking, are exactly the style of vehicle in which Confucius rode 2,400 years ago.   At the imperial capital Confucius had interviews with the keeper of the imperial archives, a semi-mythical philosopher named Lao-tsr, who founded a rival doctrine or system of mystics called Taoism ; but as Confucius himself said that he was unable to comprehend those misty teachings, and the very existence of the Taoist philosopher is largely a matter of conjecture, we need not dwell further upon this incident.*   Eighteen years ago I met the individual usually known as the Pope of the Taoist creed, who also enjoys a certain amount of imperial favour.   Of course this visit to the capital enhanced the fame of Confucius, who, on his return the same year, was regarded in much the same light as the Mussulmans regard a pilgrim to Mecca, that is, as a *haji*.   He had also taken the opportunity to improve his knowledge of music.

When Confucius was in his 36th year, a civil war broke out in the ducal dominions of Lu, owing to factional disputes with the three leading families ; the ruler was obliged to fly for refuge to the dominions of a neighbour to his north, and Confucius soon followed.   According to China's greatest historian, the origin of the civil war was a disagreement connected with cock-fighting, and it is incidentally mentioned that metal spurs were used by one of the factions.   This political quarrelling about cock-fighting has its counterpart in Europe, for it will be remembered that in Justinian's time the Byzantine court at Constantinople was shaken to its foundations by the faction fights between the red and white, the blue and green parties of the race-course and circus.

Confucius became so enamoured of the music he heard in the country of his temporary adoption that for three months he lost all zest for savoury meats.   After he had been six years in the land of Ts'i, the duke of that

---

* One of his European expositors however styles Lao-tsr " a prophet of the gentiles," because " five centuries before Christ he preached Christian doctrines."

country expressed a wish to confer a feudal estate upon him ; but one of the local statesmen—and one, too, who has left behind him a high reputation for economy and sagacity—objected, on the ground that "these learned fellows are too glib and intractable, too proud and insubmissive, too fond of showy funerals and exaggerated lamentations, too persuasive and fond of borrowing to govern a kingdom." In truth, the duke seems to have gradually become rather tired of Confucius, who accordingly betook himself once more to his native land. His disciples were now more numerous than ever. It is interesting to notice that the term which I have here translated "learned fellows" is that which is now applied to Confucianists as distinguished from Taoists and Buddhists : the term is thus older than Confucius, and seems to mean " men of parts."

It was not until his 47th year that Confucius again obtained office ; this was under a new duke, the legitimate ruler, his brother, having four years previously died in the country to which he had fled for asylum. It must be here stated that the dukes of Lu were the direct descendants of Confucius' great model, Duke Chow. A brother or a nephew had occasionally succeeded in the absence of a son ; but, with the exception of an unexplained hiatus between B.C. 920 and 855, the twenty-five dukes had regularly succeeded ever since B.C. 1122, and the reigns of the last eleven of them formed part of Confucius' own original work on history. This fact explains Confucius' great loyalty to his master, who was, in fact, a member of the imperial house, and whose ancestors were tutelary spirits on a subordinate scale. Confucius so reformed the manners of the people in the district entrusted to him that in two years he was promoted to the ministry of public works, and two years later again to that of justice. In this latter capacity he succeeded in crushing several of the haughty mesnelords, and dismantling their castles. He even went so far as to arrest and order the execution of a rich and dangerous intriguer. At the age of 52 he accompanied his master in the capacity of prime minister to a spot near the borders of the two states, and took part in an interview between his own ruler and the one who had given him hospitality for so many years. On this occasion he succeeded in defeating the insidious diplomacy of the rival state, and in forcing the surrender of disputed territory. But, though Confucius considered that a display of force should accompany diplomatic action, he took the general view that good example was more efficacious than might. Honesty, morality, and funeral etiquette advanced with such strides under the premiership of Confucius that neighbouring states began to grow uneasy. It was first thought advisable to conciliate the rising power by a cession of territory ; but wilier counsels prevailed, and a successful effort was made to corrupt the new duke's heart with presents of beautiful singing girls and fine horses. This moral collapse so distressed the philosopher that he left the country.

Now commences the period of Confucius' travels through the various feudal states, which covered a period of thirteen years. He and his disciples met with various adventures. On several occasions they were menaced by suspicious or hostile bands. On one occasion Confucius incurred the censure of a disciple by accepting (although he tried to escape it) an invitation to pay his respects to a divorced or adulterous duchess. On another he was annoyed at a local duke's relegating him to the second carriage whilst the duchess seated herself along with her husband in the first. One instance is recorded in which he distinctly broke his pledged word; but he defended himself on the ground that promises extorted by force are not binding. This saying was advanced by Chinese statesmen 17 years ago as an excuse and a precedent for repudiating the treaty made by a Chinese envoy with Russia.

Time, however, will not permit of our dwelling further upon this period of wanderings: suffice it to say that the philosopher had as many rebuffs as he had successes, and that most of the rulers, whilst willing to listen to his counsels, seemed to consider that they possessed more of an academic than a practical value. At the age of 66 Confucius heard of the death of his wife, and that his son continued weeping for her notwithstanding the lapse of the regulation period of one year. He took the view that, so long as the father was alive, crying more than twelve months for a mother was excessive. This fact, coupled with the circumstance that Confucius' grandson divorced his wife, and would not permit her son to mourn, has given rise to suspicions, owing to certain references to an ancestor made by the grandson, that Confucius must have divorced his wife. The learning upon this point is very intricate, but the best opinion appears to be that the ancestor referred to was not Confucius but Confucius' father, who had divorced, not the young girl, but the lady who gave him nine daughters; and that the philosopher was thus, not only the offspring of a strictly legal union, but true to his wife until her death.

When Confucius was 68 years of age, his own duke, son of the man who had sacrificed his reputation to horses and singing girls, sent a messenger with presents to invite the philosopher back. He went; but he neither asked for nor was offered any official post. He spent his time in composing the history of his own state, beginning with the year B.C. 722, and thus extending over about 250 years. Confucius desired posterity to judge him by this work, which, though not equal to Sz-ma Ts'ien's Book of History, published three centuries later, was in its human interest far ahead of the dry records of the then past. All Chinese history previous to this date is as vague and unsatisfactory as our own European history previous to the founding of Rome in B.C. 753. The Twelve Tables, which are the foundation of Roman jurisprudence and administrative civilisation, date from 20 years after Confucius' death; during the half century following the death of Confucius and the publication of the Twelve Tables, Herodotus went upon his travels and wrote his history. So far as my own humble researches go, I incline to compare Confucius in some respects with Herodotus, and to place exact Chinese history on a level in point of antiquity with that of Greece and Rome, and no more. Previous to the eighth century before Christ, we have skeleton annals, lists of kings, accounts of floods, and narratives of wars in the Chinese world, just as we have in the Babylonian or Egyptian world; with this important difference that, whereas in China there are no antiquities to speak of which corroborate tradition, in Egypt and Mesopotamia we have innumerable remains in the shape of buildings, mummies, and documentary evidences. Confucius attached no credence to the very ancient traditions. He used, indeed, to speak of the Emperors Yao and Shun, who lived 2,000 years before his time ; and, as we shall see, there are antiquities of that date in his temple. Then came three hereditary dynasties which lasted 1,100 years : then the imperial dynasty of which his ducal master was a scion. But, though there is no reason to question the existence of these ancient dynasties, the whole of the information amounts to very little of a practical kind.

Confucius spent the few remaining years of his life in collecting the old songs and traditions, the best specimens of which he has transmitted to us ; in fixing the principles of music, and in establishing forms, ceremonies, and etiquette. His son died four years before him, and this son's relict committed the crime of marrying again. The grandson, then 17 years of age, was carefully educated by Confucius himself, and subsequently published a system of ethics called the " Doctrine of the Mean," or Moderate, which embodies his grandfather's teachings. Confucius' declining years had already been cheered by a promise from his grandson to this effect. This grandson seems to have been a man of strong, touchy, and obstinate character ; in fact, an unpolished counterpart of Confucius himself.

One day in his 73rd year Confucius felt exhausted, and had a presentiment that death was near. His last words were the expression of regret that no intelligent rulers existed who could appreciate and utilise his services. He died a week later, and was buried just outside the ducal capital, on the River Sz, the beauty of which river had for generations been sung in the Book of Odes or Songs transmitted by him to us.

The first regular and general history of China, written by Sz-ma Ts'ien 2,000 years ago, and which in the original forms the basis of my present sketch, gives a list of Confucius' descendants down to the time when the book was completed. The great-grandson above mentioned who was not allowed to mourn for his mother died at the age of 47 ; his son died at 45 ; his son at 46 ; his son at 51 ; his son, a minister of state under the Wei kings, at 57 ; his son,—the man who hid the books in the wall when a tyrant attempted to destroy Chinese literature,—at 57. There seems to be a slight break now, for we are told that the last named had as successor a nephew almost as tall as Confucius ; this nephew, and also his son, died at 57. The son of this last was the father of K'ung An-kwoh, the man who found and deciphered the concealed books in B.C. 150, or, as the old contemporary historian says, "under his present Majesty ; and died young, leaving a son and a grandson."

We must go to other histories for facts concerning later descendants : confusion is sometimes caused by the use of such a term as 28th descendant, without specifying whether it means inclusive or exclusive of Confucius and the subject. Several served Turkish and Tartar dynasties. The 45th went as ambassador to the Kitai Tartars or Cathayans. It was the 47th who first bore a temporal or ducal title. The present duke, the 76th in descent, has just officially written to thank the Emperor for restoring to him 2,200 acres of land in Kiang Su province, granted to the family 500 years ago by Kublai Khan. It is said that one of the southern branch is about to start a daily newspaper at Hangchow, the Kinsai of Marco Polo.

The reader has now before him an outline of Confucius' life. Whilst admitting that he was a very worthy man, one fails to discover any symptoms of extraordinary genius, or any reason for the unlimited admiration in which the Chinese hold him. In his *Miscellaneous Conversations,* a book compiled by disciples, and in those later parts of the royal *Record of Rites* emanating from Confucius and his disciples, we get more precise ideas touching his character. He was a moderate eater, but very particular and nice. He was not a teetotaler, but he never got tipsy. When the mysterious forces of nature manifested themselves in the shape of storms or thunder, he considered it his duty to sit up with respect ; but he declined to enlarge upon his reasons for so doing. He always said a kind of grace before his frugal meals by offering an oblation. The oriental custom of pouring out a drop of liquor, or scattering a few grains of food before partaking of it, is still in popular vogue. Confucius' own deportment was in consonance with his teachings. He used, giving them a negative turn, almost the exact words so familiar to all Christians : he said : " What you do not wish others to do to you, do not to them." Self-control, modesty, forbearance, patience, kindness, orderliness, absence of effusiveness and passion, studiousness, industry, mildness, dutifulness, neighbourliness, fidelity, uprightness, moderation, politeness, ceremoniousness ;—these were the qualities which Confucius consistently practised and taught. He laid special stress upon the necessity of cultivating intelligence and alertness. He abominated extremes, and preached the doctrine of the *happy mean* in everything ;—in short, the doctrine of the Peripatetics ; a sort of machine-like smoothness, with no jerks or surprises, either on the side of virtue or on that of vice. Gloomy asceticism and passionate militancy were alike foreign to his taste. He was neither a theologian nor a metaphysician. He simply saw and understood his countrymen, and went to history for the means of governing them. There was nothing of the fanatic in his composition. If I wished to picture to you in life-like modern form the sort of man Confucius was, I should select an old-fashioned Quaker, such as we used to see up to 30 years ago, with broad back, bulky form ; rubicund, solid features ; ponderous gait ; and calm, gentle, peaceful, kind, but not unmanly demeanour. Yet this external or social resemblance is defective if we go below the surface : for Confucius took his liquor ; he despised women except as mothers ; that is, he granted them no such equality as do the Quakers, and he would have nothing to do with flirtations, dances, singing, sky-larking, or it may be presumed those harmless kissing amenities so popular with non-Quakers. Mencius, 200 years later, was the first to qualify him as " holy." But Confucius declined for himself the right to be called a saint, or even a good man. He said : " I am never tired of learning myself, and never weary of teaching others." He did not wish to appear censorious. Though tolerant of old religious or superstitious notions, he did not care to go into questions of future life, extraordinary things, spirits, devils, anarchy, revolution, and mystic doctrines. In the presence of the forces of nature he was, as we have seen, awed but silent ; he declined to discuss what he did not understand : he said : " Heaven does not talk, and yet the four seasons come with regularity." Some writers have gone so far as to say that pure Confucianism is no religion at all. Others describe the ancient notions, which Confucius confined himself to criticising and transmitting, as spirit-worship tending towards fetichism. What Confucius really did was to arrange ancient ideas in orderly form, and revivify them with notions of his own, just as the old Jewish teachings received fresh inspiration in the form of Christianity. The ancient idea was that there existed a Supreme Power, and that the King or Emperor, as a sort of vicegerent, was the only channel of communication with that power. In this capacity the Son of Heaven was a Mediator for his people. The worship of private families and individuals was confined to the spirits of deceased ancestors. The adorning of graves by the French on All Souls' Day is perhaps a survival of a once more universal custom. " To sacrifice to spirits not belonging to a man," says Confucius, " is mere flattery." It has always appeared to me, in short, that the Chinese regarded and still regard the next world as being a mere repetition of this, each person in this world addressing himself to those of his own rank and kind in the next. Dr. Legge is of opinion, however, that the Lordship of Heaven was, to the Chinese fathers, exactly what the notion of God was to our fathers. Confucius, like everyone else, grew up totally ignorant of any world except that in which he found himself. His prudent attitude has led some European divines to brand him outright as a sceptic, who only veiled his disbelief out of deference for antiquity. But that is going too far. He noticed that the imaginations of his fellow men led them to express belief in much that was not evident to him, so he adopted the safe course of admitting nothing but the possible existence, in a form not quite apparent to him, of sentient beings that had already lived in this world. He did not care much about the constituent elements of emotion or intellect. What is popularly known as " German philosophy " had no charms for him. It cannot even be made out whether he thought man's nature good or evil in its origin. He admits that men are naturally born different, but the effects of such initial differences are as nothing compared with the levelling effects of education and training.

Nor was Confucius inclined to split hairs upon the vexed question of sin, or even to speak of sin except in connection with the practical affairs of life. On one occasion he said that, setting aside theft and robbery, there were five capital sins,—malignancy, perverseness, mendacity, and two others not very clearly defined, but which look like vindictiveness and vacillating weakness. Confucius was a believer in the three ancient forms of divination, and an ardent student of certain mystic diagrams dating from 600 years previous to his own birth. I have never been satisfied that these diagrams had any practical meaning ; or, if they had, that the meaning now given to them by curious students expresses what Confucius really had in his mind. Confucius, in short, consulted the popular oracles, as did the Greeks and the Romans. We may disapprove, but if it was foolish to consult oracles of which he knew nothing, why should it be wiser to make requests to spiritual beings of which he also knew nothing ? The government of China still publishes a list of *dies fasti* and *nefasti*, and orders prayers to "save the moon " at an eclipse, although its officers are capable of foretelling the eclipse.   Probably Confucius fell in with popular views.   One thing is quite certain : whatever Confucius believed in a vague way as to the spiritual form which man took after death, he certainly never conceived any such idea as the doctrine of rewards and punishments. His view, concisely expressed, was that "life and death are a matter of destiny : wealth and honours are disposed by Heaven."   In other words, whilst approving individual effort, he counselled patient submission.   As he lived 500 years before our era, it is evident that he could not have believed any of our modern dogmas, unless the mystic Lao-tsz be accepted as a Christian prophet, which is absurd.   To this extent, therefore, it may be said that Confucius had no religion, and preached no religion.   Like the Persians and Chaldæans, the Chinese and the Tartars had a sort of Sabæan religion, in which worship was offered to the Sun, Moon, and Stars : at times also to other forces of nature, such as wind, the forests, and the rivers.   But these beliefs, as also that in divination, may be popular excrescences which have been superadded at a later date upon the more ancient monotheism.   Dr. Legge considers that even now this basis of monotheism is no more destroyed by popular additions than is our own monotheism by the worship of saints by large numbers of Christians. Of all the things which we, as Christians, profess to believe, there are only two things which it was reasonably possible for Confucius to believe.   He might have believed in a Maker of Heaven and Earth, in the Resurrection of the Body, and in Life Everlasting; but that scarcely amounts to a religion, as nearly all primitive men have had beliefs of this kind.   He probably did, in common with the received traditions, more or less vaguely believe in a Supreme Maker, but he did not attempt to define or dogmatise as to what that Maker was, or how he created.   He preferred to discuss the practical character of things before his eyes, and was indifferent to the causes of those things.   He says nothing about the future state, but holds that man continues, after what we call death, to live on.   The Chinese idea of death differs from ours : thus, a man may die and come to life again ; that is, may lose consciousness and revive : their ignorance of physiology precludes our absolute notion of death.   In the same way with the ghost which takes its departure on death : there is always an idea that it is hovering near the body, and may give trouble at any time if not propitiated.   There have been endless discussions amongst missionaries as to why Confucius preferred to speak impersonally of Heaven, avoiding the personal form God, and as to whether he believed in the efficacy of prayer.   In most cases the arguments appear to me somewhat biased by the personal preconceptions of the polemic ; that is to say, he wishes to prove that, if Confucius was good, it was because he believed what the controversialist believes ; if evil, because he failed to believe what the controversialist believes ; and so on.   This is, in fact, the course which the rival schools of Chinese philosophy themselves adopt.   Where Confucius is silent, they claim that he expressed in general terms the sentiments expanded by themselves.   In other words, they dogmatise.   Thus Mencius

insists that man's nature is ~~evil~~; Cincius that it is good, in its origin.   One
philosophy pleads for universal love ; another for pure selfishness.   As a
matter of fact, Confucius steered clear of all positivism ; he said, in fact,
that even his " medium policy " was a shifting medium, according to time
and circumstances : in short, he was in some respects an opportunist.   He
objected to commit himself so far as to say the dead were conscious, lest
rash sons should waste their substance in sacrifices; he equally declined
to assert that they were unconscious, lest careless sons should not sacrifice
at all.   At the same time he himself always sacrificed as though the spirits
were present.

Some blame Confucius because he was unable to grasp the full nobility
of the Taoist maxim : " Return good for evil."   Confucius took time to
consider, and finally decided that evil should be repaid by justice, and
good reserved for the recompense of good.   His own countrymen find
fault with him for glossing over, in his history, the failings of men of rank,
worth, or his own family connection ; and Dr. Legge, the distinguished
Oxford professor, shows in detail that this is true.   It is not for me to sit
in judgment upon the judges ; but I would suggest that, however noble
the precept enjoining good for evil may be when cherished in the hearts
of individuals, a government which should attempt to practise it would
soon put the business of state in a sorry condition.   Confucius was above
all things practical, and considered that confidence in the stability of the
state was more important than the adequate alimentation of the people,
which again was more vital than the possession of military strength or
learning.   He said : First enrich your people, and then instruct them.
As to the concealing of historical truths, it is hopeless to get men to agree
upon this point.   Take the modern instances of Carlyle and Cardinal
Manning : their biographers, Mr. Froude and Mr. Purcell, for telling too
much truth have received as much censure as praise.   Confucius' frame of
mind may be judged from his reply to a disciple, who was in doubt how
to act when his master, a feudal prince, was bent on a foolish act.   "Oppose
him, but deceive him not."   That is do not offend by showing your hand,
but do not conceal your hand.   What is the use of exposing the weak
nesses of those in power ?   Is it of real advantage to us that Bacon should
be proved to have been the meanest as well as the wisest of mankind ?
The Chinese idea that rulers are the vicegerents of God is tempered by.
the conviction that bad rulers may be dethroned.   Perhaps Confucius
thought it better not to rake up slumbering guilt unless it were possible to
punish at the same time.   At all events Confucius was loyal to the princely
houses, and had no axe of his own to grind : the utmost that can be charged
against him is a certain canniness which prefers to be on the safe side,
and, if it must err, then to err on the side of cold prudence rather than on
that of warm impulse.   As to mere personal defects, perhaps a testiness of
temper can be not unfairly charged against him.

It is a little difficult for us, even after stringing together such a galaxy
of virtues as we have shown Confucius to have really possessed, to understand the Chinese enthusiasm for his memory.   Our own history teaches
us to admire manly grace and beauty ; bodily activity and love of nature ;

romantic and tender attachment to the gentler sex. Whether we take military heroes such as Cæsar, Napoleon, Cromwell, Genghis Khan, Gustavus Adolphus; ecclesiastical heroes such as Thomas à Becket, Luther, Wolsey; lay heroes of statecraft such as Cicero, Sully, Talleyrand, Bismarck; philosophers such as Socrates, Marcus Aurelius, Seneca, Locke, Newton, Darwin; lawyers such as Papinian, Tribonian, Cujas, Coke; or poets such as Virgil, Dante, Shakespeare, Goethe; we find no complete character in any way resembling that of Confucius: perhaps the nearest approach is Socrates. Even the founders of our principal religions, including those of Buddhism and Muhammadanism, have very little of Confucius in their attitude; notwithstanding that in the two instances of Christianity and Buddhism the qualities which have secured the reverence of hundreds of millions are in many respects precisely the qualities possessed by Confucius. Confucius commands the regard of the European critics; but somehow it always seems that he does not secure a full measure of respect. He certainly was not a handsome man; his heavy round back, long ears, projecting teeth, and misshapen head were scarcely heroic; he disliked to discuss athletic sports; his habit of moving about in a springless ox-cart, or when on foot with his arms extended like wings, scarcely suggests perfect dignity to us; his skill as a musician would perhaps appeal more strongly to our sympathy if we were ignorant of modern Chinese music. At the same time, there is reason to believe that much of the ancient theory and science of music has been lost. It is certain that a custom existed of collecting popular ballads for purposes of government record. Many of the ancient ballads are very beautiful and simple, besides being perfectly comprehensible to the modern ear. We may therefore assume that Confucius possessed genuine bardic feeling. His treatment of women was rather contemptuous, and he says almost nothing about marriage; his love for truth was, as we have seen, occasionally tempered by prudence. His fondness for forms, ceremonies, and, above all, for funerals and mourning is not at all in our line. But here, again, a due show of grief at the loss of a parent only forms a continuous chain with the filial obedience required during life, and solemn sacrifices after death. In short, we can only account for the unmeasured reverence which Confucius has secured in the hearts of his countrymen by slightly modifying the words of Lord Beaconsfield, who remarked that "every country possessed the government it deserves," and by suggesting that China possesses the teacher she deserves; or, to put the matter into a more subjective light, by suggesting that, when a great teacher or prophet appears, the mere fact that he is recognized as a prophet or as an instrument of Heaven connotes the circumstance that he is suitable to the people who believe in him and recognize him. If we have a difficulty in appreciating Confucianism to the full, the Chinese have a similar difficulty with our beliefs, which often appear to them somewhat absurd. An able Chinese Jesuit who a few years ago published a very learned critical work upon comparative religions, thus sums up in his native tongue the attributes of Confucius: "Although Confucius taught the necessity of reverence and disinterested charity, he had no true belief in a self-existing Creator of an organized universe; no faith in promised grace to come, or in eternal life; no true love of God as a Perfect Being above and superior to all things; no true fear of God as the Supreme and Sole Ruler of the universe; and no true obedience to His command-ments." Professor Tiele of Leyden treats the worship of spirits and nature as though the ancient religion were not monotheistic; but Dr. Legge, in criticising this view, defends Confucius from the charge of animism and fetichism in their most unfavourable sense.

Others again have charged Confucius with cold-blooded eudæmonism, that is with only insisting upon virtue because it leads to temporal happi-ness. What Confucius said was "He who heaps up goodness shall have much happiness," and *vice-versâ.* I must confess I do not see anything very terrible in this; but it is evident that argument upon so abstract a point might last for ever. He declined to pray for recovery when he was sick, but he did this in such a dubious way that the commentators and the missionaries have not yet come to an understanding upon what he really thought on the subject of prayer. Dr. Edkins considers that, in the absence of Christian revelation to serve him as a guide to belief in the doctrine of rewards and punishments, Confucius did the next best and noblest thing, by maintaining the impartiality of moral retribution and the immortality of good fame. In this view he seems to be supported by Dr. Legge.

We will now quit this misty region of metaphysics, and transfer ourselves to the town and home of the Chinese philosopher, the residences of the dukes of Confucius.

The Rev. Alexander Williamson visited the spot in 1865, having first paid his respects to the home of the philosopher Mencius, who lived two centuries after Confucius, and whose descendant in the 70th generation received the traveller courteously. Dr. Williamson was less fortunate with the descendant of Confucius, who was then a youth of 16. But he saw the temple and the cemetery; and, as he passed up the River Sz, discerned about seven miles to the south-east from the city the Ni moun-tains, in a cave of one of which Confucius was born, and where there is a temple in honour of his mother. It is curious that Dr. Williamson should tell us that the modern house is west of the temple, whilst Dr. Edkins calls it east.

In 1873 Dr. Legge and the Rev. Joseph Edkins approached the cemetery (which the latter estimates at 66 acres in extent) from the north, and afterwards visited the city and temple; but they also were unsuccessful in their attempts to obtain an interview with the duke. They noticed that the poppy was cultivated even up to the birth-place of Confucius, and were disappointed to find that the wealthy duke, who increased his already large income by extensive trading, seemed to do nothing in the way of charity for his clan, not even to the extent of a university or a school. Many of the family were very ignorant and poor, and two of them actually wheeled Dr. Edkins in a barrow to the next town. But, on the other hand, the dukes have to support a large number of officers, musicians, and dancers; in fact, a petty court of their own.

Dr. Edkins published one account of the temple 13 years before his visit, and strange to say he is as self-contradictory as other visitors upon the question whether it is the palace or the temple which stands on the site of the original house.   He even says the family residence was at Mount Ni, which he places north of the tomb.

When I landed at Chefoo on the 16th May, 1869, I found that Her Majesty's Consul, Mr. Markham, had just returned from a visit to Confucius, town, and had been received by the 75th descendant, who was then 22 years of age,—evidently the same one whom Mr. Williamson described in 1865 as being a lad of 16.   The duke was diminutive in stature, and slightly deformed, but as intellectual in appearance as he was attractive in manner.   The consul was agreeably surprised at the cordiality of his reception, for even viceroys have to knock their heads nine times on the ground when admitted to an audience.   The duke's relatives were all tall fine men, and were exceedingly eager to learn what they could about Europe. The interview took place in a small study, the walls of which were lined with book-shelves : there were besides ancient manuscripts, urns, and various relics of the Sage.   Mr. Markham also visited the cemetery, a mile or so outside the city wall, and thence proceeded to the town of Mencius.

In 1893 the Rev. J. H. Laughlin visited the temple and cemetery of Confucius, but failed to obtain an interview with the present duke, the 76th in descent, who was then 21 years of age.

The city which contains the dwelling of Confucius is now called in the northern dialects K'ü-fu Hien, which, as we have said, means "Crooked Mound City."   It is stated to lie a mile and a half to the west of the ancient capital of the ducal state of Lu, whose rulers Confucius served. It is described by those who have seen it as being a small neat city, surrounded, as is customary in China, by high walls; like the walls of Chester, but more solid ; and pierced by four gates, with broad towers and guard-houses above them.   The eastern part of the city contains the temple erected to Confucius' chief disciple by the Mongols, 500 years ago. The south gate is double, which really makes up a total of five gates ; but the westernmost of the two south gates is reserved for the visits of imperial personages, and this gate leads straight up to the temple and palace, which together occupy half the city area ; that is, the northern and western quarters : the palace, which adjoins the temple, includes the site of Confucius' old house, in the hollow walls of which were concealed, in the year B.C. 212, when the so-called "First Emperor" of united China ordered the destruction of all the works on history and philosophy, a number of manuscripts and classical works.   During the Taiping rebellion of forty years ago the city was threatened, but only because the rebels wished in a general way to put all mandarins to death : hearing that the local mandarin was of the Confucian family, they did no harm to the town beyond massacring a number of people who had taken refuge in the cemetery.   The majority of the inhabitants of the city, including the executive and educational mandarins, bear the family name of Confucius, or K'ung, and there would seem to be about 20,000 of them in or near the ancestral city, and perhaps 10,000 scattered about elsewhere, chiefly in the province of Chêh Kiang, south of the Great River, whither during a period of schism the chief representative once migrated : the Golden Tartars appointed a northern-duke of their own, but the Mongols put an end to this duality.

The ducal palace, which Mr. Markham states is actually on the site of Confucius' house, is on the east side of the temple, of which the duke is always *ex officio* guardian : it and the palace together cover about 55 acres of magnificently wooded grounds. The temple is open to the public, except on the anniversaries of ducal deaths, which are locally observed as *dies nefasti*. A public thoroughfare divides the temple into northern and southern halves, most of the objects of interest being in the northern division. The palace has its own separate enclosure of high walls, and in accordance with Chinese custom is divided into courts or squares. The duke, who was surrounded by a staff of tall and exceedingly well-clad retainers, admitted Mr. Markham through the grand central gate, and in company with his guardian, lay steward, and relatives stood awaiting him in the third court: this is the way foreign officials are commonly received by Chinese mandarins ; but at one time it was difficult to make the higher ranks of them open the central gate. The dukes have estates in several of the prefectures of Shan Tung province, amounting in all to about 60,000 English acres. Besides this landed wealth, they receive a large pension from the government.

The grounds of the temple alone cover 35 acres, and are remarkable for their splendid avenues of cedar, fir, cypress, and yew trees. The southern half consists of parks or gardens, and contains many pavilions, tablets, bridges, etc. ; it has four gates. The main temple, in the northern division, is somewhat inconsistently stated by Mr. Markham to be built upon the spot where Confucius actually lived, and is composed of twelve squares, each shut off by its own massive gate and containing its own hall. The grand hall is in the third court, and stands behind a gorgeous red-roofed pavilion, open at the four sides, called the " Apricot Altar," in commemoration of a place where Confucius used to teach : twelve stone steps lead up to the platform upon which the hall is built, which measures about 100 feet deep by 150 broad, and which surrounds the hall like a verandah, leaving a margin on each side under the eaves of 15 feet : the verandah itself is surrounded by a beautifully carved railing. Eighteen white monolith marble pillars, deeply carved with dragons, twenty-five feet high, and each three feet in diameter, support the front of the great hall, which is also surrounded by a deep verandah. The total height from the ground is as nearly as possible 80 feet. Eighteen alternately black and white marble pillars support the after part, and eighteen variegated black and white marble pillars, nine on each side, make up the circuit. The hall is divided into nine compartments. The roof is of green and yellow-glazed porcelain tiles, green being used in Peking for the palaces of princes, and yellow for that of the Emperor : in the case of Confucius' temple the green predominates, although on several occasions imperial honours have been for a short period conferred upon the sage by over-enthusiastic emperors : the eaves are beautifully carved and painted, being protected by wire netting from birds; but by ancient custom the enormous number of bats which congregate in the roofs are left undisturbed. The roof is supported inside by twenty uncarved pillars of teak, each four feet in diameter, and thickly painted a bright vermilion colour. The ceiling is panelled in 400 squares, gilded and ornamented with dragons. Innumerable wooden tablets in honour of the sage adorn the roof. On a raised throne, enclosed by richly-embroidered yellow satin curtains, facing the spacious door, sits the enormous effigy of Confucius, over fifteen feet high, holding a bamboo scroll in his hand; for in his time paper had not yet been invented. On the table in front of the image are placed some of the gifts made by Emperors of successive dynasties, together with relics of the Sage. Several of the bronzes and clay dishes are over a thousand, indeed over two thousand years old; and many of the urns, enamels, and tripods are exceedingly fine. The rose-wood table actually used by Confucius is amongst the relics, together with two bronze elephants of the royal dynasty under which his ducal master nominally ruled. I must mention here that images are as foreign to true Confucianism as they are to Muhammadanism, and the interior ought in strict right to be as simple as that of a mosque; the chief Arabic inscription, in fact, occupying much the same place that the ancient Chinese name tablet does. The introduction of images into Confucian temples is a Buddhistic innovation, and simply marks one of the numerous compromises between the two cults; but it is not permitted to place images of the Sage in Buddhist or Taoist temples: in the case of Confucius the regulation tablet is placed above the image, and is marked " the resting-place of the Holy Sage Confucius' spirit." Most of the carved black marble slabs which panel the hall are in imitation of the Buddhist style, and represent scenes in the philosopher's career. One of the slabs, however, contains a portrait said to have been taken during Confucius' life, but it is now very indistinct. In this same hall are statues of Confucius' son, grandson, twelve favourite disciples, and Mencius; and at each of the two sides of it, in the courtyard, are rooms, seventy-two in all, in honour of each disciple. Each of these persons has a history, some Emperors adding to, others reducing, the numbers of those qualified to share in the worship rendered to Confucius, or to his system of philosophy.

The other halls in the temple precincts are in honour of Confucius' father, of whom there is an image; his mother and wife, to whose memory there are tablets; his son and grandson; Mencius; and the four leading disciples, all with tablets only, in orthodox style. The remains of an old cypress or juniper-tree, planted by Confucius himself, are shown; also the well out of which he drank, and a very much worn slab of black marble giving a genealogical tree for the 77 generations. The temple was built over a thousand years ago, but has of course been frequently repaired, the last time according to Mr. Markham in 1864, or since that date. However, I have in my possession an official letter from the Governor of Shan Tung to the Emperor, stating that it had been repaired in 1869, the very year of Mr. Markham's visit. About ten years ago part of the palace was burnt down, but the officials and gentry of China soon subscribed a sum to rebuild it.　In the correspondence upon the subject it is stated that the buildings destroyed were built about 1550, and repaired about 1840.

I have tried my best to give an intelligible description of the great Confucian temple.　For the information of those who have been in China, I may add that it is like any other large temple, especially like those of the Ming Dynasty Tombs near Peking, but on a vaster and more magnificent scale.　There is almost no architectural variety in China.　There are innumerable other antiquities and objects of historical interest, not only within the precincts of the temple and palace, in the city, and in the immediate neighbourhood, but in neighbouring cities, and all over the province, which of all Chinese provinces, is perhaps archæologically the most interesting ; but I have only undertaken to write ;a paper upon Confucius, and space compels me to narrow and confine myself to that one subject.

There still remains the cemetery, which is on the banks of the River Sz, a good mile to the north of the city, from the gate of which runs for 2,600 yards a noble avenue of two thousand old cypress or cedar and yew-trees, planted at intervals, about 500 years ago, by the Ming dynasty.　Of course these trees are emblematic of immortality or imperishability.　The road is beautified by numerous bridges and honorary portals, more, however, for ornament than to serve any useful purpose.　Half-way up the avenue are two handsome' pavilions, erected 300 years ago by the last Chinese dynasty.　The cemetery, described 1,000 years ago as lying between the Rivers Sz and Chu, $\frac{1}{3}$ of a mile from the older city, is a densely-wooded enclosure of 50 acres, surrounded by high walls : the only gate is on the south side.　A writer of the 5th century gives the then area as 16 English acres.　For some unexplained reason the avenue of pines which runs north towards the tomb does not run directly from the gate, but turns round at a point a hundred yards or so from the gate to the west. This second avenue is lined on each side by stone figures of lions, elephants, leopards, unicorns, camels, and two human figures.　At the north end of the pine-tree avenue the road turns west, and the second avenue begins where the road divides, at a small historical stream called the Chu, or Red River, into two bridges.　Ordinary visitors are directed to dismount here, as they would do in approaching an imperial edifice.　The easternmost bridge leads to the modern cemetery, in which each member of the six or seven thousand existing Confucian families has a right to be buried.　The heads of the clan alone have mounds and stone figures : the others mere slabs.　The western bridge leads to a large hall, without image or tablet, in which the family offer sacrifices twice a year, and the back door of which faces the tomb.　The tomb enclosure is walled off from the general cemetery above mentioned, and contains only the graves of Confucius, his son, and his grandson.　These are simply three mounds covered with brushwood, those of the son and grandson being west and east in front, and that of the philosopher occupying the further or north-west corner.　The Sage's mound was described 1,400 years ago, as being 50 feet by 75, and 12 feet high.　It is now about thirty-five feet in diameter and twenty feet high ; in front of it are a carved stone table, a stone urn, and a stone tablet 25 feet high, the last inscribed in ancient character with the words "the most holy sage and princely disseminator of literature." To the west is a neat but modest little house built to commemorate the reed hut in which Confucius' most faithful disciple (the one who painted his portrait, as will appear later on) mourned for his master six years.

Readers of Marco Polo will remember that he often speaks of burning the dead in China. Buddhist priests are still cremated, but Confucius was properly buried, in accordance with the patriarchal customs then prevalent over the greater part of north and west Asia.

Confucius' own reigning duke set up a great lamentation for him when he died, and it is (somewhat doubtfully) said erected a temple to his memory for quarterly sacrifices of a bullock; but no word of panegyric beyond the bald expression " Father Ni " was conferred upon his memory. The royal or imperial dynasty took no notice whatever of his death. The people of the ducal state, who came from time to time to pay their respects to his memory, gradually formed a village round the tomb, and such relics as the Sage's hat, clothes, cart, lute, and books were preserved in what seems to have been the shrine, or, if there was no temple, then in a museum or other commemorative building. During the disturbed period B.C. 225-200, when the old royal house gave place to usurping emperors, and the feudal system was practically abolished, Confucius' memory naturally grew dim ; but the founder of the celebrated Han dynasty, which was the first truly historical dynasty to really rule over a united China and to open up political relations with Western Asia, personally visited Confucius' grave in B.C. 195, and offered an ox, a hog, and a sheep to his memory ; this is exactly the *suovetaurilia* of the Romans ; that is, a sacrifice of a *sus*, *ovis*, and *taurus* at what were called lustrations. About B.C. 145 a regularly constituted temple was erected at the Sage's village, but apparently not by an Emperor. Several other emperors of this dynasty and of the subsequent branch known as the Later Han, took part in honouring Confucius, either by building temples, or by personally sacrificing to him and his disciples at the village or the tomb; or, again, by conferring titles upon him. It is curious to notice that his first official posthumous title dates from the year A.D. 1, when the Emperor added the word "Disseminating" to "Father Ni"; this was changed by the founder of the Wei dynasty in A.D. 242 to the word "Holy." In the last quarter of the first century of our era music was introduced at the worship, and a century later, after the introduction of Buddhism, an image of the Sage was added. During the first half of the third century the temple underwent extensive repair at the hands of the local ruler, acting under imperial commands issued by the northern dynasty of Wei. China had now been split up into three separate empires, but was reunited towards the close of the third century : the founder of this new unifying Tsin dynasty ordered quarterly *suovetaurilia*, both at the imperial capital and at the village. In the fifth century China was again divided into northern and southern empires. Though the northerners were Tartars of nomadic origin, they it was who first erected a Confucian temple in their capital, which was near the Tenduc of Marco Polo's time ; and they also conferred a new title upon the philosopher.

It had now become the custom of women to visit the tomb in order to pray for children, but the Tartar rulers prohibited this vulgar practice. Confucius' birthplace seems to have been in the dominions of the southerners, for the Nanking emperors rebuilt the temple, and added six bands of musicians, thus placing the sage on a footing with his prototype the Duke of Chow, to whom Confucius was so fond of pointing as a model, and whose grave lies near his own. About the middle of the sixth century there were rapid changes of dynasty in the north, and the founder of the Ts'i house of Tartars, who owed his empire partly to his obsequiousness towards the rising Turkish power, ordered Confucian temples to be erected in every first-class city, with monthly sacrifices. The great conquering Chinese dynasty of T'ang in the seventh century once more reunited the empire, and drove out the Tartars. After being degraded to a rank below that of Duke Chow, Confucius was confirmed by the T'ang dynasty in his title of " Holy Man," both words, " Holy " and "Disseminating," being added to "Father Ni " in A.D. 637. Temples were now ordered in all towns even of the second and third classes. The third emperor of this dynasty meddled a great deal with Confucius' titles and privileges, amongst other things depriving him of his *taurus*, and leaving him only *suovilia:* after this monarch's death, his usurping wife, the Chinese Catherine II., also conferred a separate title of her own upon the philosopher. Early in the eighth century Confucius was promoted to the rank of " Literature Disseminating Prince or King "; provided with a robe and crown ; made to face south like a royal personage, instead of east as hitherto ; and given precedence over the Duke of Chow.

A number of ephemeral Turkish or Tartar dynasties intervened between the fall of the Chinese T'ang house and the rise of that of the Chinese Sung. As may well be imagined, the Turks did nothing at all for Confucius. In A.D. 960 the founder of the Sung dynasty, the southern branch of which ruled over the so-called Manzi empire of Marco Polo, substituted clay figures for the wooden ones which had hitherto been used. About fifty years later the Emperor once more changed the title of Confucius, besides conferring high posthumous rank upon his father (who was given a special shrine), his mother, and his wife : in A.D. 1012 the same Emperor once more modified the title to what it long remained, *i.e.*, " Most Holy Literature Disseminating Prince." In 1083 Mencius was associated with the Confucian worship : but we are not treating of him now. In the year 1102 the son and grandson of Confucius were made posthumous marquesses, taking their titles from the Rivers Sz and I. The idea was that the Marquess of the Sz should protect the cemetery from the inundations of that river.

The Cathayan Tartars ruled over Mongolia, Manchuria, and part of Peking province, but they are not recorded to have noticed Confucius in any way ;—although, after his raid upon the Turko-Chinese capital in 946, the second Cathayan Emperor died, on his way home, at a place not very far to the west of Confucius' village. In 1031 Confucius of the 45th generation was sent as envoy to the Cathayans, who had the bad taste to invite him to a theatrical farce in which the sage came on the boards in a comic character. Confucius the 45th very properly left the theatre. Soon after this the Tungusic ancestors of the Manchus, known as the Golden Tartars, overcame the Cathayans and conquered North China ; the Sung or Manzi were driven across the River Yangtsze. The term *mantsz* means "uncouth ones"; it was and still is given by the northerners in retaliation for the contemptuous term *tatsz*, or Tartars. Both northern and southern emperors made changes in the temple ritual. The true duke seems to have followed the fortunes of the Chinese or southern emperor, who quartered him in the city of K'ü-chou Fu in Chêh Kiang province, where to this day a number of the family remain. In 1103 the purely temporal ducal title now borne by Confucius' lineal representatives was finally confirmed : it had been first conferred in 1055, but was slightly modified in 1086. Thus the ducal title may be said to date from our William the Conqueror.

The Golden Tartars were displaced by the Mongols, who soon absorbed the Manzi empire as well, besides Persia and Russia. In 1220 Genghiz Khan sent all the way from Afghanistan to fetch a Chinese Taoist philosopher from his native village, which lay to the east of Confucius' town ; but he does not seem to have been at any time struck with the Confucian sentiments. In 1281 Kublai Khan even deprived Confucius of his title of "holy," and reduced it to that of "mediocre sage"; but, immediately after Kublai's death, his grandson and successor Timur ordered that Confucius should be once more universally worshipped. He built a Confucian temple at Peking in 1306, and his successor Hayshan renewed the "Most Holy" and "Princely Disseminator" titles, with the addition of the words "Very Perfect." In 1330 the Emperor Jagatu or Tu Timur conferred upon Confucius' father and mother the title of "Prince and Lady Introducers of Holiness"; a year or two later his wife also received a high posthumous rank.

A Buddhist priest founded a new Chinese dynasty in 1368, and ordered half-yearly sacrifices to Confucius : in 1382 he further ordered the orthodox wooden tablet to take the place of earthen images ; but painted clay images, clothed and hatted, seem to have been decreed once more in 1410. In 1476 eight bands of musicians and other additions were made to the ritual. In 1499 a fire partially destroyed the temple. In 1530 it was decided that to place Confucius on a level with Heaven was a mistake. His royal title was taken away, and that of "Most Holy Former Master" substituted. It was argued that, Confucius never having been a prince when alive, it was absurd to make him one posthumously ; moreover, that "Disseminator of Literature" was inadequate to express the sage's qualities. The term "temple" was ordained in place of "palace hall," and clay images were once more abolished in favour of the simple tablet. The bands were reduced to six, and other technical modifications instituted. Notwithstanding these alterations, no great change has been made in the ceremonial arrangements at the tomb, which, as we have seen, are of semi-imperial nature ; as, for instance, in the case of the 25 foot column marked "Disseminating King."

The first Emperor of the reigning Manchu dynasty in 1644 confirmed

Confucius the 65th in descent in all his family privileges and titles : the tablet was inscribed "Very Perfect Most Holy Literature Diffusing Former Master Confucius," that is, it renewed Hayshan's precedent minus the word "prince" or "king." Every city and town was commanded to possess a temple, and the highest civil official was enjoined to conduct the worship. However, the Sage's family were ordered under pain of death to wear the Manchu pigtail and official costume, like any other mortals. A Confucian temple was established at Moukden, the capital of Manchuria. In 1651 an officer was sent to sacrifice at the Confucian village, and in 1652 the Emperor himself sacrificed at the Peking Academy. In 1657 it was decided to omit the words "Very Perfect" and "Literature Diffusing," these terms being as vain an effort to qualify Confucius as it would be to limit the universe or measure the light of the sun and moon ; thus reverting to the precedent of 1530, which still holds good. The youthful Emperor reported to the *manes* of Confucius the date of his entrance upon the higher classical studies, and gave the equivalent of £10,000 sterling towards the repair of the family temple. The work was duly announced to the spirits as having been completed in 1660.

In the seventh year of his reign the second Emperor sacrificed to Confucius at the Academy. On this occasion the military officials were for the first time made to take part. In 1684, acting under the suggestion of the Board of Rites, his Majesty called in person at the village on his way back from Nanking. He dismounted from his chair at the temple gate of the inner court, proceeded on foot up to the image, and *kotowed* nine times. An officer was despatched also to sacrifice to Confucius' father and canonised ancestors. The hereditary Duke K'ung Yü-k'i showed the Emperor about, and explained that the existing image was ascribed by tradition to the date A.D. 541 : the name of the artist was Li Yen, [and I may add the then reigning Tartar Emperor Gholugun was father of the founder of the Ts'i dynasty above alluded to]. The Duke showed some sacrificial objects actually deposited by one of the Han Emperors in A.D. 85 ; also the lithograph of Confucius as Chancellor, from the drawing of the celebrated artist Wu Tao-tsz of the 8th century ; the sage's table, his seal, and several other images or lithographs. The portrait most like Confucius was declared by the Duke to be the small picture of the sage followed by one of his disciples : this was actually sketched by another disciple, Tsz Kung, from life ; but it was redrawn or retouched by the famous draughtsman Ku K'ai about the fourth century of our era. The Emperor left his yellow umbrella with a crooked handle to be placed amongst the imperial relics. It was explained to his Majesty that Confucius actually taught where the Apricot Altar stood, and that the two ancient characters there were written by one Tang Hwai-ying of the Golden Tartar dynasty. Many other historical calligraphies were exhibited. The old juniper-tree planted by Confucius himself was stripped of its branches and leaves at the fire of 1499 ; but the trunk looks like and is as tough as iron, whence it is popularly known as the "iron tree." After visiting the library, containing all the books given by successive dynasties, the Emperor inquired if there were any vestiges of the old house, and was informed that part of the old wall was still in existence, just behind where the Emperor was then standing : the exact place where Confucius' son was twice stopped by his father to answer questions about his studies was also indicated by the Duke. The Emperor tasted some water from the old well, and, asking for further information touching the old hollow wall, was informed as follows : When the First Emperor was burning all the books in B.C. 213-212, the ninth descendant concealed copies of the chief canonical works in the wall. About B.C. 150 the feudal duke of the old state undertook some repairs, and whilst engaged in extending the temple, or palace as it was then called, the workmen heard the tinkling of musical instruments inside the wall. Search was made, and a number of bamboo books were found. Although there is still some vagueness in the Duke's words, it would thus seem that the old house was east of or behind the hall containing the statue, and that the well belonged to the house.

After explaining all this to the Emperor, the Duke accompanied his Majesty to the cemetery, the latter descending from his horse at the bridge we have mentioned, and walking up to the grave, before which he *ketowed* thrice. The pines, acacias, and "quartz-crystal" trees growing upon the mound were explained to have been brought by the disciples from their own districts, and the names of them were mostly unknown. The Duke said the total area of the cemetery was from 270 to 300 acres, and that there was now insufficient space for interments. When the Emperor got back to Peking, he wrote a wooden tablet and also a poem on the old juniper tree, to be engraved on stone and placed in the temple. The latter seems to have been actually sent in 1687. In 1686 a decree announced that 160 acres of land should be added to the cemetery, and that it should be freed from taxation : this gift partly explains the discrepancy between the 16 acres of the 5th century and the 50 acres of Mr. Markham. Confucius the 66th, or whatever his number was, would probably not waste the land given to him, but, like any other Chinaman, make it pay until required for use as a burial ground. The Emperor commanded that in future military mandarins should always assist at the half-yearly worship : censors were ordered to watch the ceremony, and to call anyone, the Emperor included, to book if inattention were shown. For several years after that the Emperor showed in various ways his interest in the village temple worship, and in 1693 entirely renovated the shrine.

The third Emperor rebuilt the temple much as we now see it, a fire having again destroyed it in 1724. A new image was made and clothed in garments sent by the Emperor himself. The name of the Five Ancestors' Temple was modified.

It has been the practice ever since for each Manchu Emperor on his accession to write a few complimentary words to be transferred to a wooden tablet, the Duke keeping the original manuscript. In 1857 the seventh Emperor placed Confucius' half brother among the honoured ones. The present Emperor on his accession 22 years ago sent the four written words "Truth is lodged here," referring to an utterance of the philosopher when threatened by a hostile mob. The Duke sent up an obsequious memorial offering to come to Peking to offer his congratulations, and his offer was accepted.

In addition to the chief temple at the village of the sage, there are, apart from the 1,500 city temples attached to the district examination halls, five others of a higher order. These are at the seat of the schism or emigration in Chêh Kiang; at a place a day's journey from Shanghai in Kiang Su; in the Peking Palace; in the old Tartar capital of Shan Si; and in the western province of Sz Ch'wan.

Some of the Europeans who have visited the temple at Confucius village have described the ceremonies and the worship, but it does not appear that any have actually seen them performed: at Shanghai, and perhaps at other of the treaty ports, foreigners have witnessed the local sacrifices, which are of course on a smaller scale; but in every instance the chief civil authority, accompanied by the military subordinates as well as his own, acts as a sort of high priest; but this term is not approved by Dr. Legge, whether applied to the Emperor or to others. A slow time dance, something after the fashion of our minuets, is performed by fifty youths, and meanwhile the six bands, each of six players, discourse shrill music. The airs are the same as those played in Confucius' time. The *suovetaurilia* and other symbolical offerings stand on tables between the incense vase flanked by two candles upon the altar and a roll of spotless white silk spread out upon the floor, the last ready for burning before the Sage's tablets, after the departure of the spirit. But the offerings are mere expressions of devotion, in no way intended as expiations of sin. The high priest arrives at dawn, and is supposed, as in ancestor worship, to have fasted and contemplated for three days. The adoration which I saw offered to the Emperor of Annam in the spring of 1893, with its hymns, kneelings, and knockings, seems to correspond in most particulars, with the exception of the dance, to the worship of Confucius. Accordingly, the fact that in China, and the states of her subordinate neighbours, the so-called worship is offered to the living as well as the dead points to a radical divergence of idea, and exemplifies once more that these ceremonies approach rather the Byzantine idea of lay adoration than the Christian sentiment of religious worship. Confucius was as far as possible from regarding himself as a prophet, not to say a god. In using the expression " Heaven gave birth to what virtue is in me," he distinctly recognises himself as a created being, and owing duty as such to a higher than himself. To a certain extent he considered himself to be an instrument or expounder of this higher being. No prayer is offered to Confucius, nor is his assistance sought in any way; and, as we have already shown, a Tartar dynasty 1,400 years ago prohibited the vulgar innovation, then being introduced by barren women, of seeking his mediation in their favour. Confucius is simply worshipped as one who codified learning; as a sort of re-embodiment of the Duke of Chow, civil founder of the first truly historical imperial dynasty, whose memory was worshipped in Confucius' time both at the imperial and ducal capitals, and whose tomb still lies near to that of Confucius. The worship offered to the Duke of Chow was simply a repetition of that which had always been offered to the *manes* of China's best Emperors, who were what Sir Henry Maine describes in ancient western history and law as simply the *Themistes* or Assessors of the Deity, whether called Zeus or Ti. Or the sacrifices may be regarded as being made to them as earliest inventors or founders. Thus, one is worshipped as the founder of agriculture, another as the discoverer of the silk-worm, and so on. When we come to think of the importance of writing in the world, we have less difficulty in revering Confucius as a discoverer of records and history.

SPECIMEN OF CONFUCIUS' HANDWRITING.

In the margin is a specimen of the handwriting of Confucius that has been retraced in later times. The following photo-lithographed facsimiles of eight pictures are taken from a Chinese book on Confucius.

LIST OF SUBJOINED PICTURES.

1. The mother of Confucius prays at Mount Ni for a son. Confucius' forehead was like Mount Ni. Hence his name Ni, the Second.

2. Confucius as a lad playing at sacrificial services, and imbuing other boys with his spirit.

3. The Duke sends two carp as a present when Confucius' son (hence named "Carp") is born.

4. Confucius, accompanied by two young pupils of rank, visits the imperial capital, and seeks instruction on points of form from the mystic philosopher Lao-tsz (Lao-tsé).

5. Confucius orders the execution of a rich scoundrel.

6. The Duke of Ts'i sends a present of dancing-girls to the Duke of Lu, who falls into the trap and neglects duty.

7. A messenger from Lu statesmen induces Confucius to hasten back to his native land.

8. Confucius staggers to the door. Presentiment of death.

因上生尼母一年同尼
名圩尼尼頃十賀岑彦山
字頂子嫂是兵年公致
仲象既明而足以年之禱
尼尼生尼生于年乃降之九

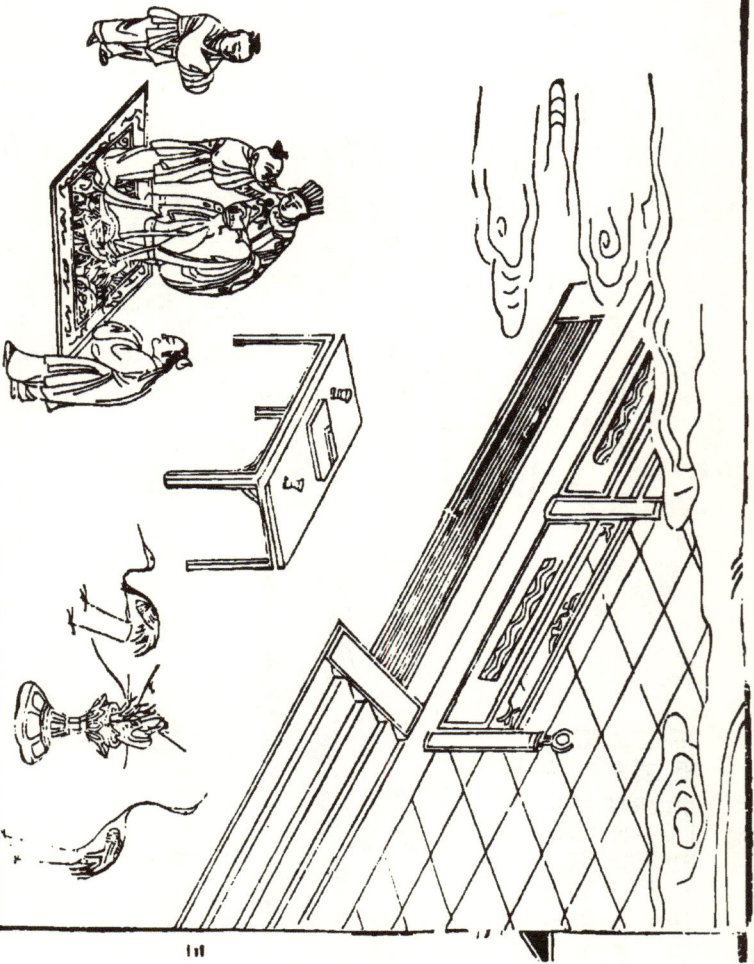

挺是性兒兄孔祖
遠墨不淌過權于呂
名兒學與咨戲五盧
聞化而至與常藏六
列效能天同嫫載泰
國相他相嫫姐兩
與由其邃且羲

字名柴魚孔命
伯其君鯉鯉子名
魚曰其君子之生生娶
亶故孔子以于鯉

闕孔子觀乎明堂睹四門墉有堯舜之容桀紂之象而各有善惡之狀興廢之誠焉又有周公相成王抱之負斧扆南面以朝諸侯之圖也孔子徘徊而望之謂從者曰此周之所以盛也

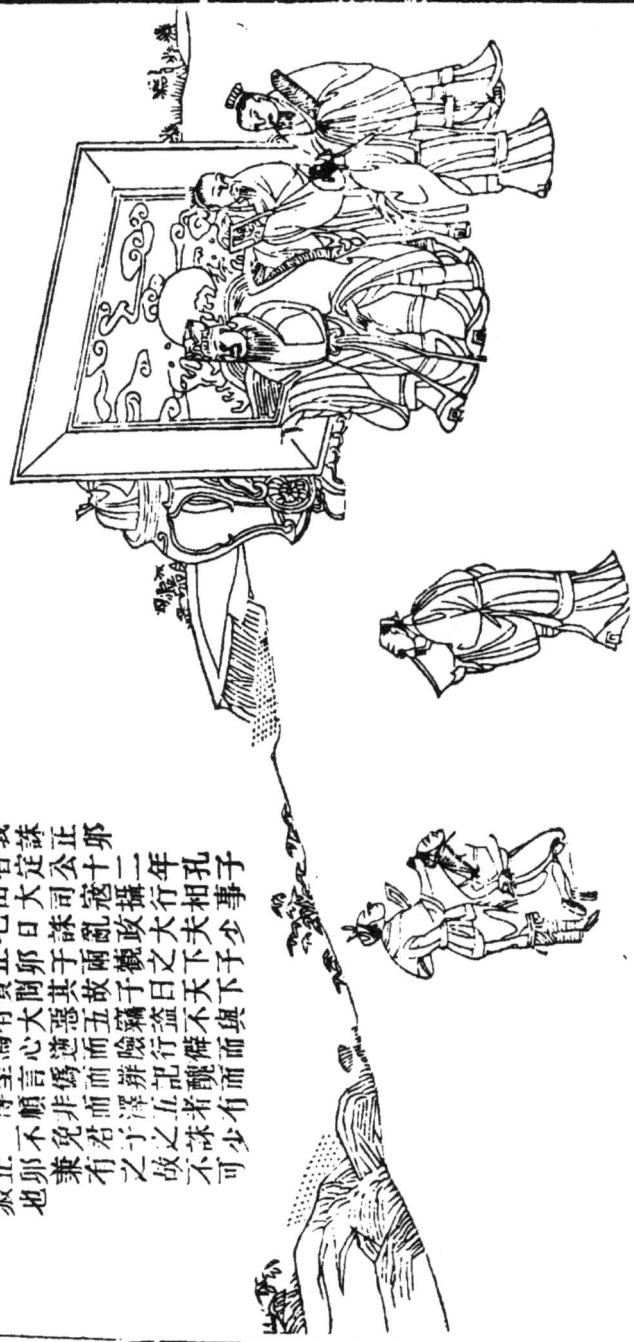

救正一博壑喬實有賈正七由啓義
他卯不順言心大閭邪日大定誅
兼免卯而偽遂惡惡其誅司公正
有若而而五故兩飯政寇十邪
之寸洋辟陰險竊政年二
故之五記行益行之大
不誅者醜而解不夫天下夫相孔
可少有而與天下子少事子

因齊人歸女樂以沮孔子
由以孔子遂行以此去魯
齊之君臣以太牲分去
其政齊君臭聞遊子孔會
過事齊樂太高
因子為馬子故
夫陋周三人棋
聯不道十七將
訊怒遊劉人霸

四十

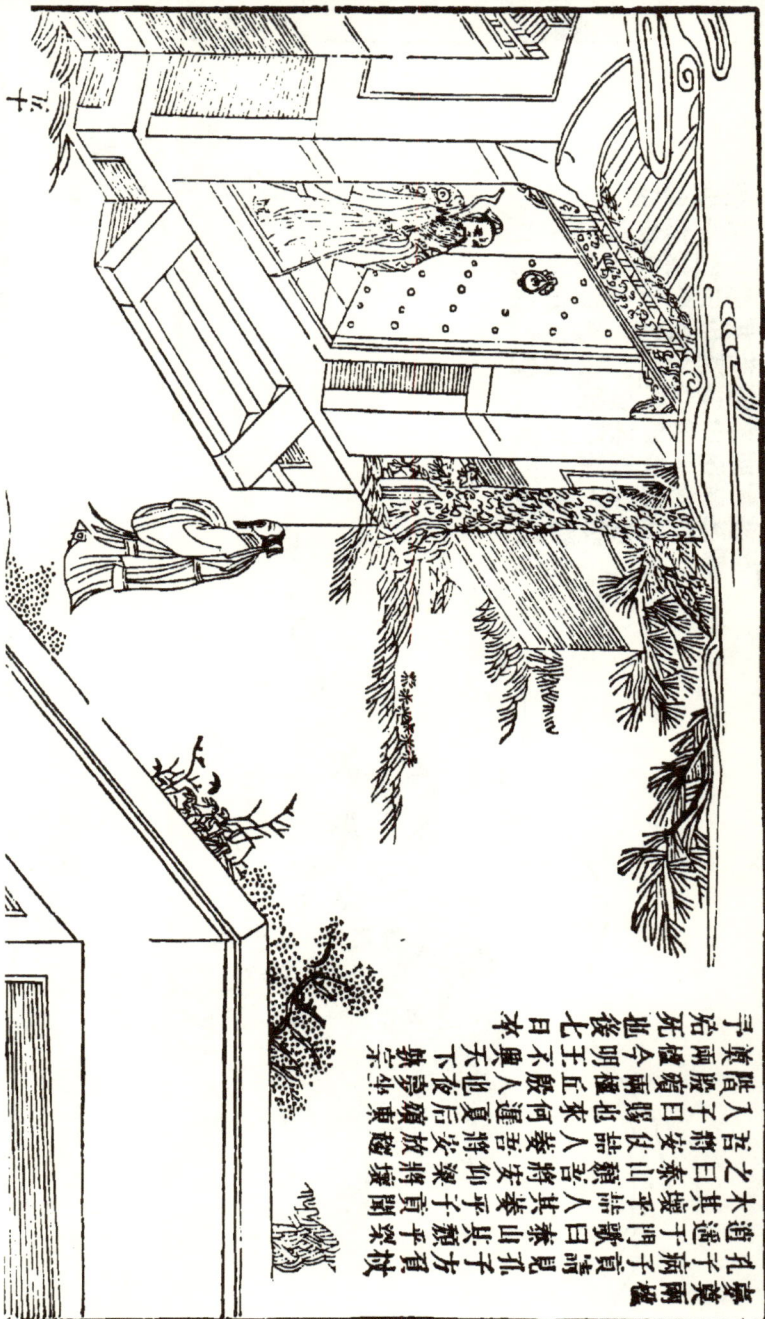

于寝門入而哭之大道孔子蚤
祐兩楹殯日安坐于梁木其壞
進今一而病且七日不食矣夢
七王丘來何夢坐奠於兩楹之
日不殆後人葬仰於兩楹其哲
天也后殷將死兮夏后氏殯於
下殆夏於殯將萎乎泰山其頹
夫華東楹之間孔子殆將病子貢

www.ingramcontent.com/pod-product-compliance
Lightning Source LLC
Chambersburg PA
CBHW032143080426
42733CB00008B/1185